MW00666993

LIVE YOUR DREAM

To my father, father-in-law, and grandmother, all of blessed memory; to my wife and kids; to my extended family of coaches, teammates, and friends; and to all kids who have learning challenges. —T.G.

To my father, Gary, for the push he gave me to be great at whatever I chose to be. —J.M.

Thanks to Yisroel Teitelbaum for the photograph that inspired the image of Tamir shooting a basket on pages 20–21.

PJ Publishing creates board books, picture books, chapter books, novels, and graphic novels in multiple languages that represent the diversity of Jewish families today. By sharing Jewish narratives, values, and life events, we help families explore their connections with Jewish life.

All rights reserved. No part of this publication may be reproduced, distributed, or transmitted in any form or by any means, without the prior written permission of the publisher.

For information regarding permissions, please email permissions@hgf.org or contact us at:
PJ Library, a program of the Harold Grinspoon Foundation
67 Hunt Street, Suite 100
Agawam, MA 01001 USA

First published in 2025 by PJ Publishing, an imprint of the Harold Grinspoon Foundation.
Text copyright © 2021 Harold Grinspoon Foundation
Illustrations copyright © 2023 James Madsen
First Edition. All rights reserved.
No part of this publication may be reproduced, distributed, or transmitted in any form or by any means.
Designed by Michael Grinley
0125/B2760/A7
ISBN 979-8-9891668-8-6
Library of Congress Control Number: 2024931577
Printed in China
Manufactured for: Harold Grinspoon Foundation, 67 Hunt Street, Suite 100, Agawam, MA 01001

LIVE YOUR DREAM

The Story of a Jewish Basketball All-Star

by Tamir Goodman
illustrated by Jim Madsen

Tamir’s ball bounced off the rim.
His brother Reuven grabbed it and dribbled around him.
Swish! Reuven scored the winning points.
Tears streaked Tamir’s cheeks. He had lost again.

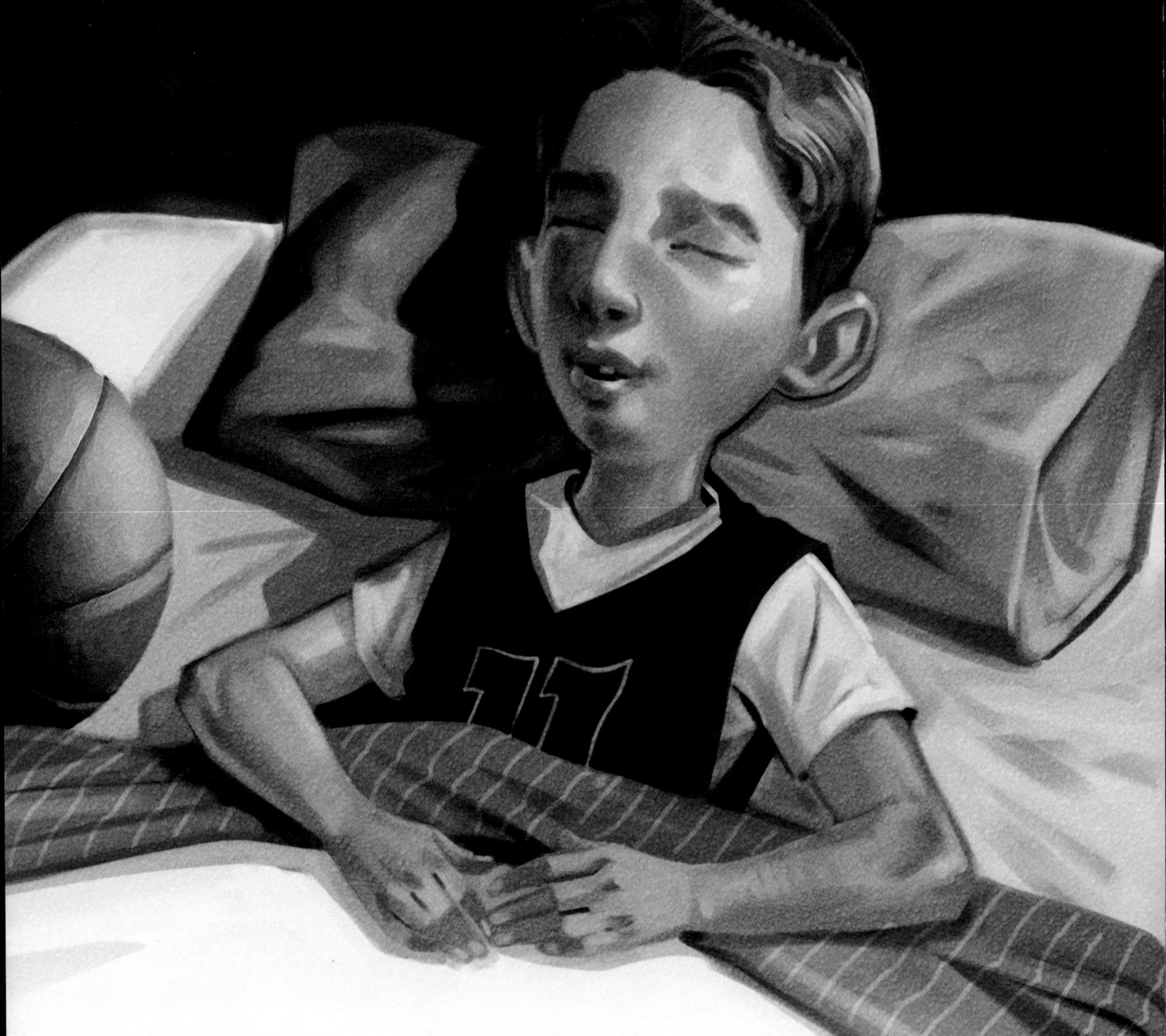

Even so, Tamir couldn't wait for the next pick-up game. He thought about basketball day and night. He wore a basketball jersey to bed. He dreamed that someday he'd be a professional basketball player.

When Tamir talked about his dream, his mother gave him a special smile. More than anyone, she understood he was serious.

Each week, Tamir's big family observed Shabbat, the Jewish Sabbath. They enjoyed a special meal on Friday night and attended services at their synagogue on Saturday. As Tamir listened to the Torah being read, he felt proud to be Jewish.

From sundown on Friday night until three stars appeared in the sky on Saturday evening, the end of Shabbat, Tamir prayed and rested.

In kindergarten, Tamir entered the Talmudical Academy of Baltimore. When he tried to learn to read, he found it impossible. Letters seemed to change places, like the players on a basketball court. Left became right and right became left.

If Tamir couldn't read a word, he substituted a different one in its place. Because reading was so difficult, Tamir tried to avoid it. He acted like a clown in class and often asked for a bathroom pass.

"The kids at school think I'm stupid," Tamir told his mother and father. "But inside, I know I'm smart."

His parents hired a tutor to help Tamir with his homework each morning before school started. Harold Katz, the school basketball coach, invited Tamir to study at his house.

“Take your time, don’t rush, and write the way you speak,” Coach Katz advised.

Even though Tamir’s reading and spelling improved, he continued to struggle with schoolwork.

Finally, in high school, Tamir was diagnosed with dyslexia.

"Your brain is built differently from other people's," the doctor explained. "That's why you have trouble decoding words.

You told me you love basketball. Dyslexia might be a problem in the classroom, but I'm sure it has helped you on the basketball court."

It was true.

On the court, Tamir could picture in his mind where his teammates were located. He could tell in seconds who would be open for a pass, even before the player himself knew it.

22

Tamir worked hard on his basketball skills as a point guard.

In one game, the score was tied.
Tamir grabbed the ball in midair and laid it into the net for the game-winning points. He pumped his fists in the air as the crowd roared.

In the car on the way home, his father said, “Basketball is a blessing, and you made a great shot. But remember, it’s important to practice humility. Don’t let success go to your head.”

Tamir never forgot those words.

His fans eagerly watched Tamir as he dashed onto the court.
They gasped as he drove the ball with lightning speed into the net.
They cheered as he shot a ball backwards and scored.
They leapt to their feet as he made his 35th point.

Little did they know that Tamir couldn't read the scoreboard. He had to ask his teammates which team was winning.

TALMUDICAL
22

The more Tamir played, the more his game improved.

He learned that he couldn't control the game by questioning a referee's calls. It was more important to focus on what he could control — drills, showing respect, and teamwork.

He discovered that if he had a bad game, it should not affect his self-esteem. It was better to move on and try to play better next time.

At age 17, Tamir was ranked the 25th-best high school player in the country. The top US sports magazine, *Sports Illustrated*, wrote an article about him. They called him the "Jewish Jordan," comparing him to famous basketball player Michael Jordan. Major TV sports networks invited Tamir to appear on their shows. In one week alone, he received 700 requests for interviews.

Tamir had become a celebrity.

It was difficult to deal with all the attention, but he remembered his father's lesson about humility. "Don't let success go to your head."

Talmudical Academy's gym was too small to hold Tamir's fans, so in his senior year, Tamir switched to Takoma Academy. A Christian Seventh-day Adventist school, it had an excellent basketball team and a large gym.

Best of all, it treated Saturday as a day of rest. Unlike most other schools, its teams did not play on Friday nights or Saturdays. Tamir could be part of the team and still observe Shabbat.

Tamir made lots of friends.

He liked his teachers.

He continued to excel at his favorite sport.

Tamir had to make a decision about college.

The University of Maryland had invited him to join their top-ranked Division 1 team. Although they tried to change their game schedule to honor Tamir's rule of not playing on Shabbat, they were unable to do so.

Soon afterward, Towson University, which also had a Division 1 team, offered Tamir a basketball scholarship. He was thrilled to accept their offer when he learned they'd honor his Sabbath rule.

22
50
92

At Towson, Tamir achieved good grades. Their basketball team won more games than they had in recent seasons. But after a year and a half, an amazing opportunity came along that Tamir couldn't ignore. Maccabi Tel Aviv, the top professional basketball team in Israel, invited him to join them.

His dream had come true!

Tamir moved to Tel Aviv. Over a period of seven years, he played for four different teams in the Israeli league.

Tamir loved living in Israel.

He was with people who practiced their Jewish faith.

They understood his Sabbath rule.

And he could spend time with his safta, his grandmother.

While playing in Israel, Tamir had several serious knee and hand injuries. He took time off to recover, sometimes for up to a year, before struggling back to the court. His injuries, however, finally made it impossible to continue playing professionally.

At age 27, Tamir had to retire. He was deeply disappointed. After all, he had lived and breathed basketball his whole life.

Tamir thought about how he had overcome obstacles that had stood in his way. Then a lightbulb went on in his head.

Even though I can't play professionally anymore, I can share everything I've learned with young players!

Tamir quickly got to work. He set up basketball clinics and camps for children and teens all over the world.

"You don't have to be perfect," he tells young players. "Struggles can lead to success. Just do your best and remember that you're important, even when you don't play well."

Today, Tamir continues to travel extensively, teaching, coaching, and encouraging children to live their dream, just as he has always lived his.

TAMIR GOODMAN
BASKETBALL CA
JERUSALEM 5'8

IMPORTANT DATES

January 18, 1982
Tamir is born into a big family in Upper Park Heights, Baltimore, Maryland.

Fall 1987
Tamir starts kindergarten at Talmudical Academy of Baltimore, where he struggles with reading. Harold Katz, the school coach, helps Tamir with his homework and becomes a lifelong advocate and friend.

1998
In 11th grade, Tamir is diagnosed with dyslexia. On November 17, he receives an offer from the University of Maryland to join its Division 1 team on a basketball scholarship after graduating from high school.

January 29, 1999
Tamir is ranked the 25th-best high school player in the United States.

February 1, 1999
Sports Illustrated publishes a four-page profile on Tamir.

September 1999
Tamir transfers to Takoma Academy, a Seventh-day Adventist school, in Takoma Park, Maryland. He declines the University of Maryland's offer after learning that, despite best efforts, they can't accommodate his Sabbath rule.

April 12, 2000
Tamir is named Most Valuable Player of the Capital Classic, an "all-star" annual basketball showcase for high school seniors. Many participants go on to become NBA players, some making it into the Basketball Hall of Fame.

September 2000
Tamir enters Towson University in Towson, Maryland, on a basketball scholarship, joining its Division 1 team.

Spring 2001
Tamir makes Towson University's Dean's List and receives a Coach's Award for exceptional performance on the court and in the classroom.

July 22, 2002
Tamir signs a three-year contract with Maccabi Tel Aviv, Israel's top professional basketball team.

September 2002–June 2003
Tamir is loaned to Givat Schmuel, a professional Israeli basketball team.

August 13, 2003
Tamir marries Judy Horowitz. They go on to have five children.

August 2003–June 2004
Tamir plays for Elitzur Kiryat Ata, a professional Israeli basketball team. He injures his left knee and undergoes physical therapy.

June 2004–June 2005
Fulfilling a requirement for all Israeli citizens, Tamir serves in the Israel Defense Forces, where he specializes in armed personnel carriers and receives an Outstanding Soldier Award. During this time, Tamir also suffers another left knee injury, resulting in major surgery and nine months of physical therapy.

2005–2006
Tamir plays again for Givat Schmuel and reinjures his left knee, resulting in nine months of physical therapy.

December 2007
Tamir moves back to Baltimore to play for the Maryland Nighthawks, a newly formed professional team in the Premier Basketball League. He suffers a complex dislocation of his right-hand finger, resulting in major surgery and a year of physical therapy.

July 2008
Tamir signs with Israeli professional basketball team Maccabi Haifa and moves back to Israel. During practice, he shatters several bones in his left hand, has six months of physical therapy, and is unable to play for the rest of the season.

June 2009
Tamir moves to Cleveland, Ohio, and enrolls in online courses at the University of Maryland to finish his college degree.

August 2009
After seven years of playing Israeli basketball and multiple injuries, Tamir retires.

December 2012
Tamir receives a BA in Communications from the University of Maryland. He begins coaching and getting involved in educational and charity work.

December 17, 2013
Tamir publishes his first book, *The Jewish Jordan's Triple Threat: Physical, Mental, and Spiritual Lessons from the Court*, co-written with his wife, Judy.

2013
Tamir invents SportStrings Tzitzit, a compression-fitted jersey for Jewish players, and Zone190, a training device used by NBA teams and many basketball athletes.

August 26, 2014
Tamir moves to Jerusalem and launches a Jerusalem-based basketball camp for young players and NBA coaches/personalities.

January 2021
Tamir co-founds Aviv Sports, LLC, which develops new products such as the Aviv antimicrobial and moisture-wicking basketball net.

GLOSSARY

Antimicrobial: The absence or reduction of germs on an object.

Division 1: The highest level of competition in college sports.

Drills: Repetitive training exercises in basketball and other sports.

Dyslexia: A condition that makes it difficult to learn to read, spell, and interpret words, letters, and other symbols.

League: An association of sports teams that organizes matches for its members.

Physical therapy: Special care and exercises to relieve pain and build body strength.

Pick-up game: A nonprofessional game that is for fun or practice.

Point guard: A basketball player that dribbles, passes, and scores. The point guard also defends against the point guard on the opposing team.

Safta: Hebrew for "grandmother."

Scholarship: A grant or payment to help pay for a student's education.

Seventh-day Adventist Church: A Christian church that observes Saturday as a day of rest.

Shabbat: The Jewish day of rest that starts at sundown on Friday night and lasts until three stars appear in the sky on Saturday night.

Swish: A basketball dropping through the net without touching the rim or backboard.

Torah: The first five books of the Bible.

Tzitzit: The tassels or fringes on garments that some Jews wear to remind them of specific commandments.

Wicking: When perspiration is removed from a fabric or object.

INVENTIONS

Tamir never slows down. Besides training young basketball players, he lectures, scouts, and invents. Below are descriptions of three of his remarkable inventions.

SportStrings Tzitzit

A basketball jersey that is designed with two layers of material and satisfies requirements of Jewish law. The inner layer is made of a high-performance athletic material that is anti-odor and antimicrobial. The outer layer is made of cotton, has most of its sides open, and has tzitzit on its four corners.

Zone190

For three years, Tamir purchased simple plumbing fixtures and experimented with them in his garage. After much trial and error, he discovered that if he stretched a trampoline-like material across a 190-degree carbon-steel frame, he could make the device shoot balls at players from different angles. Zone190 is an excellent training device for basketball players because the varying angles are the same as in a live game.

Aviv Net

During the Covid-19 pandemic, Tamir invented a basketball net that cleans off germs and sweat from the ball's surface after it is shot through the hoop.